Y0-ASO-186

TO GOD BE THE GLORY

Other books by the Author:

The Preaching of Bishop John Bryant
100 Ways of Empowering Women

TO GOD BE THE GLORY

A Celebration of the Life of
Bishop Frederick Calhoun James

by

Rev. Dr. Mankekolo Mahlangu-Ngcobo

GATEWAY PRESS, INC.
Baltimore, MD   1996

Copyright © 1996 by Rev. Dr. Mankekolo Mahlangu-Ngcobo
All rights reserved. Permission to reproduce in any form must be secured from the author.

Please direct all correspondence and book orders to:
Rev. Dr. Mankekolo Mahlangu-Ngcobo
3315 Mondawmin Avenue
Baltimore, MD 21216

Library of Congress Catalog Card Number 96-75560

Published for the author by
Gateway Press, Inc.
1001 N. Calvert Street
Baltimore, MD 21202

Printed in the United States of America

DEDICATION

*To men and women everywhere
who are willing to be used by God*

CONTENTS

ACKNOWLEDGEMENTS ix
INTRODUCTION xi

Chapter 1 1
HIS CHILDHOOD
"Unto us a child is born; unto us a Son is given."
—Isaiah 9:6

Chapter 2 5
CALL TO THE MINISTRY
"How then can they call on Him in whom they have not believed?...How can they hear without a preacher?"
—Romans 10:14

Chapter 3 9
THERESSA GREGG
And the Lord God said: *"It is not good that the man should to be alone; I will make him a help meet for him."*
—Genesis 2:18

Chapter 4 17
RENEWING THE MINDS OF HIS PEOPLE
"Study to show thyself approved."
—II Timothy 2:15

Chapter 5 23
THE OFFICE OF A BISHOP
*"If a man desire the office of a bishop,
he desireth a good work."*
—I TIMOTHY 3:1

Chapter 6 33
A MISSIONARY TO SOUTHERN AFRICA
*"Go ye therefore and teach all nations, baptizing them in the
name of the Father, and of the Son, and of the Holy Ghost."*
—MATTHEW 28:19

Chapter 7 53
A SOLDIER FOR JUSTICE
*"The Spirit of the Lord is upon me...
to liberate the oppressed."*
—LUKE 4:18

Chapter 8 59
ECUMENICAL INFLUENCE
"One Lord, one faith, one baptism."
—EPHESIANS 4:5

Chapter 9 61
HEALING THE SECOND EPISCOPAL DISTRICT
"With his stripes we are healed."
—ISAIAH 53:5

Chapter 10 71
THE MINISTRY BEYOND THE SANCTUARY
*"And there are diversities of operations,
but in the same God which worketh all in all."*
—I CORINTHIANS 12:6

Bibliography 79
About the Author 81

ACKNOWLEDGEMENTS

I would like to give thanks to Bishop Frederick Calhoun James and his lovely wife, Dr. Theressa Gregg James, for allowing me to enter their personal lives to write this book, and to Miss Wilhelmenia Miller, Bishop's secretary for providing me with the materials I needed. I would also like to thank the committee that wrote *African Methodism in South Carolina, the Bicentennial Focus*, under the leadership of Bishop James, and also the committee that produced the video of Bishop Frederick C. James, "The Visionary Leader." They both provided information which made this book easier to write.

I would like to thank Roslyn Campbell for typing my manuscript and also Evelyn Ward and Glenn McNatt for reading and editing it. Thanks to Rev. Mamie Williams, Pastor of Hughes Memorial United Methodist Church who provided me with other materials. I would also like to thank the presiding elders and ministers in the Second Episcopal District for their contributions. Finally, I would like to thank my daughter Ntokozo for her patience and support.

INTRODUCTION

On January 10, 1995, I attended the reception in honor of Bishop and Mrs. Frederick Theressa James, for the 50th anniversary of their ministry to God's people and also of their marriage. The reception was organized by the Baltimore African Methodist Episcopal (AME) ministers' conference and was held at Bethel AME Church on the corner of Druid Hill Avenue and Lanvale Street, in Baltimore, Maryland.

I sat in the back of the hall and was able to see everyone who attended the celebration. I witnessed the radiance on the faces of the ministers. I felt the spirit of joy and amazement at Bishop and Mrs. James' accomplishments. Speaker after speaker congratulated them for being obedient and faithful to the ministry of our Lord Jesus Christ and for having been married for half a century. What a blessing! I was moved by the prevailing Spirit, the sweet, sweet spirit that prevailed in Coker Hall and was inspired to write a poem entitled "50 Years of the Jameses." As I wrote, I felt the need to write the story about how God moved in the life of Bishop Frederick James with Theressa Gregg James at his side. It is a story that should be told to everyone who needs to hear and be inspired, for it is no secret what God can do.

Researching the lives of the Jameses was informative and inspirational. In this book the reader will learn about the childhood of Bishop James in Chapter One. In Chapter Two, I relate how he was called to the ministry. Chapter Three deals with Theressa Gregg, his life partner, wife and dear friend. In Chapter Four, I describe his ministry in education, renewing the minds of his people. How his ministry took him to the Episcopal office he desired is the subject of Chapter Five. Chapter Six, deals with his leaving his homeland as a missionary to southern Africa. Chapter Seven, tells how he fought for political and economic justice. His ecumenicalism is described in Chapter Eight. Chapter Nine discusses his work in conflict resolution, as a healer who united the Second District of the AME Church. In Chapter Ten, I describe the visionary bishop who understood that Jesus not only ministered in the synagogue, but went to the sea, to the mountains and valleys to preach, teach and heal the broken hearted, and to find the lost through his ministry beyond the sanctuary.

After reading this book, you will join me in saying: For the things He has done with and through Bishop James and Theressa Gregg James, **"TO GOD BE THE GLORY."**

1

His Childhood

"Unto us a child is born, a son is given."
Isaiah 9:6 (KJV)

Frederick Calhoun James was born on April 7, 1922 to Rosa Lee James, a church pianist and her husband, Edward James a mechanic and baritone singer in Prosperity, South Carolina, a small community with a population of 844, in Newberry County.

Young Frederick James' birthplace was well named because many black people in Prosperity owned property which they shared with other family members. The extended family was honored and respected. The Jameses lived next door to Frederick's maternal grandmother, Clara Gray, his grand-aunt, Sally Young, and her daughter, Nancy Bridges. Each owned a house.

Frederick James grew up in a house filled of music. His mother played the piano at their family church, Shiloh AME, Church which also had a primary school where Frederick

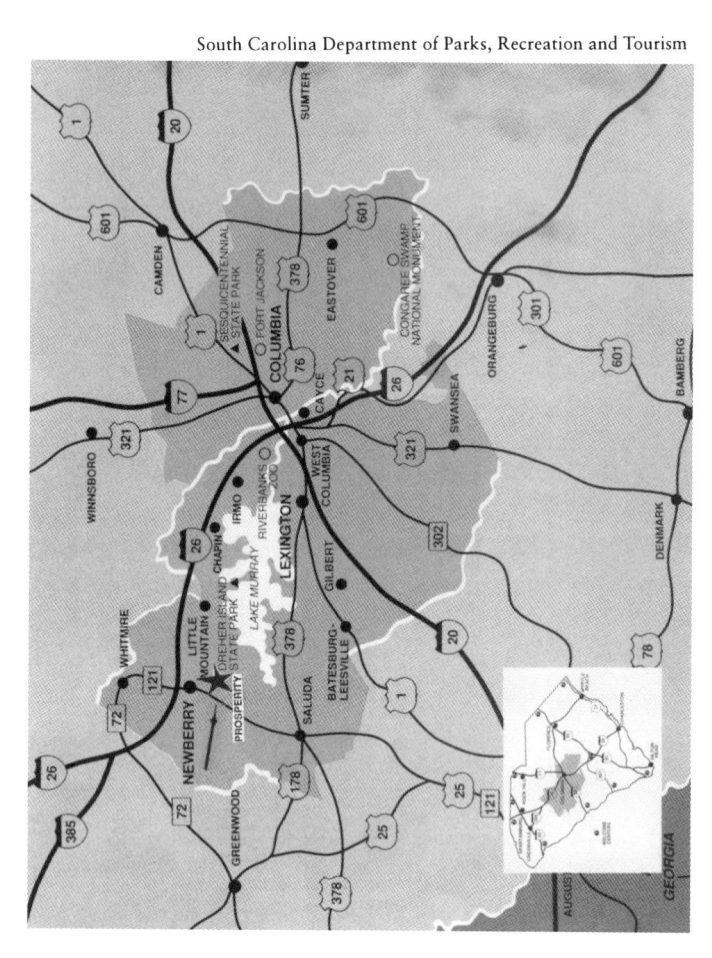

South Carolina Department of Parks, Recreation and Tourism

Map of South Carolina, showing Prosperity, birthplace of Frederick Calhoun James (see star).

attended classes. Frederick's father was a hard working mechanic, at the railroad yard in Newberry. Frederick was reared with a strong work ethic. He was taught that a man has to work in order to earn money to support his family, that work builds self esteem, and that if one worked, one would not be a beggar. Frederick's family also emphasized education. He was taught to read at an early age, and quickly fell in love with books, newspapers and magazines. He discovered that reading increased his knowledge of his surroundings and of the world.

Frederick also learned the value of self help at a early age. He started to work early, selling blackberries and blueberries at five cents a bag. Later, he also sold peanuts and newspapers. At nine, Frederick opened his first bank account with $3.00. In those days $3.00 was a lot of money—especially for a child.

Frederick also performed odd jobs to make money. He cut lawns and later he worked as a chauffeur for a rich white man in Newberry. With his entrepreneurial spirit, Frederick thought he might be a successful businessman, but God had other plans for him.

While Frederick was working odd jobs to make money, he also was attending school. After elementary school, he went to Howard Junior School for the ninth and tenth grades, then Drayton Street High School in Newberry for the eleventh and twelfth grades. In 1939, at the age of seventeen, he received his high school diploma with honors. From high school, Frederick went to Trenton, South Carolina to attend Bettis Junior College, where he played football, and received an

Associate Degree. He then entered Allen University, an institution of higher learning in South Carolina founded and operated by African-Americans. The school was based on philosophy of African Methodism, under the auspices of the African Methodist Episcopal Church. At Allen University, Frederick became editor of the school newspaper, *The Allen Journal*. He also worked as a waiter at the local hotel to pay his college tuition. He graduated from Allen University in 1943, cum laude, receiving a Bachelor of Arts degree.

2

His Call to Ministry

*"How can they call on Him in whom they have not believed?
...How can they hear without a preacher?"*
ROMANS 10:14 (KJV)

Frederick James had always wanted to be an entrepreneur. Making money and becoming a big businessman in South Carolina was his goal. But while still a teenager, he had become fascinated by the discovery of God within himself while attending Sunday School and church at Shiloh AME. The wonder of the birth of Christ and the forgiveness of sins through Christ confirmed in him the great love of God for people. Frederick had many questions. He wanted to know God more and more as he grew older. Once he even asked his pastor about the call to ministry. His pastor discouraged him, saying he was too young and that he should wait until he was older before making any decision. The call to preach continued to burn in his heart. However, finally in 1943, at 21, he decided to leave his pursuit of his business to pursue the business of the Heavenly Father. After graduating from

Allen University in Columbia, South Carolina, he was licensed to preach by Presiding Elder W. B. Loving Clark. The following year, December, 1945 he was ordained a Deacon together with Frank Madison Reid II by Bishop Frank Madison-Reid Sr. at Bethel African Methodist Episcopal Church in Columbia, South Carolina. He then left South Carolina to attend Howard University School of Religion in Washington, D.C. The now Rev. Frederick James became assistant minister at Metropolitan African Methodist Episcopal Church, the Cathedral of African Methodism, under the Reverend J. Beckett. At Howard, James also showed his leadership skills, becoming involved with many organizations on campus.

He graduated from Howard University in 1947 with honors, receiving Bachelor of Divinity (B.D.), the equivalent of the Master of Divinity (M.Div.), cum laude. Reverend James' first ministry was as pastor of Friendship AME Church in Irmo, South Carolina, which he was called to in the summer of 1945. He was also pastor of Bishop's Memorial AME Church in Columbia, South Carolina during the summer of 1946. After completing his divinity studies at Howard University, Rev. James was called to Wayman AME Church in Winnsboro, South Carolina where he served from 1947 to 1950. During this time he was teaching philosophy, religious studies and the Old Testament at Allen University.

In 1950, Rev. James was assigned to serve as a pastor of Chappelle Memorial AME Church in Columbia, South Carolina where he served for three years.

As an itinerant minister in the AME Church, Rev. James was assigned to be a pastor of Mt. Pisgah AME Church in

Sumter, South Carolina in 1953. There, through his preaching, vision, commitment and zeal, he revived the church to spiritual renewal and social transformation. He carried the mission of Christ as written in the gospel of Luke Chapter 4 verses 18-19 (TEV). "The spirit of the Lord is upon me, because he has sent me to proclaim liberty to the captives and recovery of sight to the blind, to set free the oppressed and announce that the time has come when the Lord will save his people."

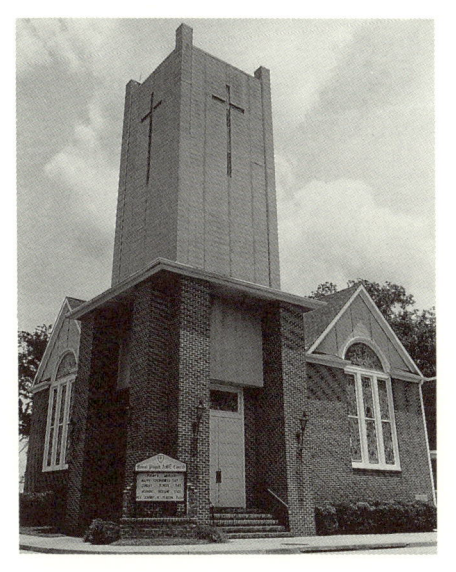

Mt. Pisgah AME Church in Sumter, South Carolina

Chaplain James A. Holmes Jr. in his article "AME Bishops Born in South Carolina and AME Bishops Elected from South Carolina," in the book *African Methodism in South Carolina — A Bicentennial Focus,* writes:

Rev. James built Mount Pisgah into one of the great pulpits in America. James razed the old Mount Pisgah and rebuilt it into its former historical structure. He built the James Village, one of the first churches to support housing projects in South Carolina. A great pulpiteer, when he preached, he combined inspiration with the intellect. His sermons feed the souls and the mind.

Rev. James served Mt. Pisgah for almost twenty years, until 1972, when he was elected the 93rd Bishop of the African Methodist Episcopal Church.

Surely the Lord has breathed on Rev. James to tell the world about His love, grace, forgiveness and justice. For over 50 years he carried the call to his ministry.

3

Theressa Gregg

*"It is not good that the man should be alone,
I will make him a help meet for him."*
GENESIS 2:18 (KJV)

Theressa Gregg, a petite, beautiful, intelligent, non-materialistic young woman, came to Allen University to further her studies. She was from Marion, South Carolina. Her parents Mr. and Mrs. Gregg, raised her in a religious atmosphere. Her early education was at Marion County Training School. She completed her freshman and sophomore years at Kittrell College in Kittrell, South Carolina, then entered Allen University to earned a Bachelor of Arts degree in history.

At Allen, she took the same course in which Frederick James had enrolled. One morning, Professor T.V. Swinton called Fred James to draw a map on the black board. James went with confidence and drew the map. Professor Swinton asked if the class was satisfied with James' presentation and illustration. Theressa Gregg, raised her hand and questioned the position of one of the cities on the map. Professor Swinton called Ms. Gregg to point the discrepancy on the map. She went to the black board and drew the map with every city in that country as it appeared in the book. She also revealed the city which Frederick James did not put in the right position on the map. James looked at her and was impressed by her intelligence.

Dr. Theressa Gregg

After the class, James went to talk to her. James asked her if she needed a friend, someone to protect her on campus. She accepted and that was the beginning of the love story now over fifty years. They both graduated from Allen. She graduated cum laude.

From Allen University, Theressa Gregg went to Columbia University in New York City to study education. She completed her master's degree in education and became a teacher. Rev. Fred James and Theressa Gregg were married by Dr. Charles Leander Hill on December 30, 1944 at the parsonage of Bethel AME Church, Columbia, South Carolina. The union of the two people, Frederick James and Theressa Gregg was what God intended in the completion of Genesis 2:18. "I will make a suitable companion to help him." The Jameses became a model Christian couple.

Theressa became a teacher at Marion County Training School in Marion, S.C. She also taught at Waverly Elementary School in Columbia, at Liberty Street Elementary School and Centroll School, both in Sumter and was an assistant principal at Liberty Elementary School.

Mrs. James worked diligently with the missionary society in the local churches where her husband was pastor. In the AME Church, pastors' wives assist with the missionary society, either as president or advisors.

The Women's Missionary Society is a connectional organization of the African Methodist Episcopal Church. The purpose of the missionary society is:

- to help women and youth to grow in the knowledge and experience of God through Jesus Christ
- to seek fellowship with women in other lands
- to initiate and maintain the support system
- to create opportunities and resources to meet the needs of women and youth
- to fulfill the responsibility of the mission of the church, home and overseas

The Society encourages every woman to become a missionary. As more women entered the ministry, the society has also welcomed men in order to include the women ministers' husbands. *(Book of Discipline)*

Theressa Gregg understood her role as the First Lady of the church when she married Rev. James. As Rev. James excelled in building the local church, Mrs. James excelled in building the Missionary Society and the Young People Department (YPD). She became the YPD Director of Columbia Conference branch and later the 7th Episcopal District YPD Director.

When Rev. James was elected Bishop in 1972, Mrs. James stopped teaching to join her husband in southern Africa. She travelled with him to every District. As a supervisor of a District she was able to organize local missionary societies in the District. She was sensitive to women without shelter, and started a project to buy blankets for the needy during the winter, and to raise money for missions locally and abroad. In the Second District, the missionary society under her leadership in 1995 raised $90,000 in two and half months at Heritage Institute under the leadership of Ms. Shirley Sheeres. Mrs. James' dedication to missions earned her an honorary doctorate in Humanities from the University of Monrovia, Liberia in West Africa in 1988.

Tireless, humble, serious looking Mother James is an asset to Bishop James, and the church. She knows her husband well as a man who places the needs of the people before his own. She was able to master that quality and respected it. Bishop James describes his wife as "honest, open, idealistic, fragile, easy to please, an excellent teacher, intelligent and trustworthy." She is loving, caring, sincere and warm. Although the Jameses did not have children, they were able through their ministry and mission to be a mother and father to the motherless and fatherless in churches, at home and abroad. Truly, this couple has been joined together by God. It is not surprising they have spent their lives together as husband and wife, for more than 50 years!

Mrs. Christina N. Chambliss, the former Second Vice-President Connectional Missionary Society states:

> Our Supervisor, Dr. Theressa Gregg James made a deep impression on our Missionary Society in the 2nd District, with new emphasis on the substance of the work of missionaries within the structure and framework of our organization. Her consistency and adherence to duty are well demonstrated. Her spirit and sincerity have given us a challenge and the will to continue our work and become more dedicated to our commitment to God and to each other.

Mrs. M. Cynthia Douglass, wife of Presiding Elder Douglass states:

> Dr. Theressa Gregg James is a true servant of the Lord. She gives witness to the Lord by sharing unselfishly of her talent, stewardship and discipleship to all whom she comes in contact with. She gives wise counsel to the clergy spouses, promoting fellowship, sisterhood and brotherhood. She has led efforts in skillfully executing projects in the Second Episcopal District such as paying off the balance of the AME homeless shelter in Raleigh, North Carolina, the blanket project for Church World Services and her continued commitment to the work in South Africa.

Dr. Theressa Gregg James has been a member of other organizations outside the AME Church. She is a member of Church Women United, Bishop's Wives Council, Alpha Kappa Alpha Sorority, Governing Board of the National Council of Churches of America, Church World Service Committee and National Council of Churches.

In all these organizations she is the servant of God and the people. Side by side with her husband, Bishop James, she works everyday in the Second Episcopal office on a small desk and she is effective.

This is the poem I wrote as they celebrated fifty years in ministry and in marriage:

FIFTY YEARS OF BISHOP FREDERICK JAMES

WITH

DR. THERESSA JAMES

by

Rev. Dr. Mankekolo Mahlangu-Ngcobo

Fifty years of two hearts filled with LOVE.

Fifty years of partnership in FAITH.

Fifty years of the two who responded to GOD'S CALL.

Fifty years of MINISTRY and MISSIONS.

Fifty years of two GREAT MINDS in ONE.

Fifty years of MOUNTAINS and HILLS climbed.

Fifty years of VALLEYS and RIVERS crossed.

Fifty years of PAIN and CRIES.

Fifty years of POWER and VICTORY.

Fifty years of EMPOWERING GOD'S PEOPLE LOCALLY AND GLOBALLY.

Fifty years of walking in SPIRIT and in TRUTH.

Fifty years of MERCIES and MIRACLES.

Fifty years of PATIENCE and PASSION.

Fifty years of BLESSINGS and BLESSINGS.

PULA NATTE, PULA MME.

KHOTSO NTATE, KHOTSO MME.

MORENA A HO HLOHONOLOFATSHE (SESOTHO)

TO GOD BE THE GLORY!

Bishop and Mrs. James

4

Renewing the Mind of his People

"Study to show thyself approved."
II TIMOTHY 2:15 (KJV)

Bishop Frederick James understood early on that mediocrity is not acceptable and that knowledge is power. At Allen University, he learned the history of the university, and began to understand God's mission through Daniel Alexander Payne of South Carolina. Daniel Payne had purchased his freedom and was concerned about the minds of the black people who were horribly oppressed throughout the South. In 1870, Bishop Brown and the Columbia District Conference purchased land and built a school, Payne Institute, named after this pioneering educator. The school became Allen University in 1880.

Frederick James taught at Allen University and at Dickerson Theological Seminary while serving as pastor at Chappelle AME Church. He was the dean at Dickerson Theological Seminary from 1949 until 1953, and during that time he challenged the minds of his students in philosophy and in Old Testament studies. Even as a young scholar, Rev. James knew how to engage in theory at Allen, as well as practice at Chappelle AME Church. As a Dean at Dickerson Theological Seminary he was in charge of the seminary as well as four extension schools in the region. The Seminary offered Bachelor of Theology (B.Th) and Bachelor of Divinity Degrees.

Dean James, educated many pastors who went on to do great things in their churches. He encouraged students to study hard, always reminding them that education was a privilege not to be taken lightly and that, in 1835, a law had been passed in South Carolina which made it a crime to teach black men to read and to write. But, Daniel Payne continued to teach and was forced to flee to the North to escape prosecution.

Dean James insisted his students could be anything they wanted to be. He was strict, straightforward, disciplined and scholarly, and he made the seminary one of the best schools in South Carolina.

Many Dickerson alumni who are leading ministers today recall Dean James as their inspiration, mentor, father and role model. As a teacher and scholar, he pursued excellence at Dickerson and left a legacy for future generations. Dean James in a sense became the Daniel Payne of the 20th century, a man dedicated to renewing the minds of his people.

In 1984, Bishop James was assigned to lead the Seventh Episcopal District in South Carolina. In that year, Allen University was doing poorly and some thought it was doomed to close its doors forever. Enrollment had decreased to a few hundred students. There were only ten full-time faculty members and the school had lost its accreditation from the Southern Association of Colleges and Schools in May, 1978. Between 1974 and 1984 eight presidents had tried to lead the university out of its desperate plight but all had failed. The school was $3.8 million in debt. In July, 1984 Bishop James became the Chairman of the Board of Trustees at Allen proclaiming "Allen University will rise again." *(South Carolina District, Special Issue)*

Bishop James and the Allen University Trustees immediately initiated a search for a new University president, with vision and faith. Dr. Collie Coleman, who holds a doctorate in higher education administration from Ohio State University was appointed president on July 28, 1984. Together with Bishop James, he began the long hard task of resurrecting Allen University. A partnership among Bishop James, Dr Coleman, the board of trustees, the South Carolina AME Church, faculty staff, students, and Alumni Association of Allen University (AAAU) was formed. The leadership of Bishop James and Dr. Coleman motivated and inspired the people to give to the cause. Between 1940-1991, the annual giving increased from $10,000.00 to $210,000.00 The University was enabled to pay its bills. Faculty and staff were added. The enrollment of the University increased. Over a period of few years, the campus was rejuvenated, buildings were refurbished and painted *(SCD S Issue)*.

Allen University applied for accreditation from the Southern Association of Colleges and Schools (SACS). On Friday,

Chappelle Administration Building

J. S. Flipper Library

Gibbs Science Hall

June 19, 1992, at the Summer meeting of the Southern Association of Colleges and Schools in Norfolk, Virginia, Allen University won unconditional accreditation. Bishop James, Dr. Coleman, and the Allen community held a Praise and Thanksgiving Service on Wednesday, June 24, 1992. The work continued. Between 1984 and 1992, members, Missionaries Young People's Department, and laity in the Seventh District raised seven million dollars for Allen University. The commitment to renew the minds of the people was again demonstrated at Allen University. *(SCD S Issue)*

S.C. Movers and Shakers

There is no consensus on the most influential or powerful people in South Carolina, but here are a few of the nominees for the elusive list:

Bob Royall — Banker

Jim Waddell — Senate Finance Chairman

Roger Milliken — Industrialist

Bill Gibson — NAACP President

Fred James — AME Church Bishop

Robert McNair — Former Governor

Bob Sheheen — House Speaker

Dick Riley — Former Governor

Carroll Campbell — Governor

Max Lennon — Clemson President

5

The Office of the Bishop

"If a man desire the office a bishop, he desireth a good work."
I TIMOTHY 3:1 (KJV)

The mission and ministry of Rev. James at Mt. Pisgah AME Church grew in leaps and bounds. His ministry transcended the sanctuary and touched the societal ills in South Carolina, echoing the connectional of the African Methodist Episcopal Church.

At this point Rev. James decided to become a bishop so his ministry could extend from the local church to the Episcopal District, and the church as a whole. He had already authored the 1960 Social Bill, which created the AME Commission on Social Action. He was a member of the General Board of the Church and his name was known and respected throughout the connectional as the first director of the Commission on Social Action.

At the 1972 General Conference in Dallas, Texas, Rev. James was elected the 93rd Bishop of the African Methodist Episcopal Church. Bishop James became the first bishop elected to the Episcopal office from a pulpit in South Carolina.

As Bishop James' first charge was to lead the Fifteenth Episcopal District, which included the Cape Province of South Africa and Namibia. During that period, he also was asked to take charge of the Eighteenth Episcopal District, including four countries namely, Lesotho, Swaziland, Botswana and Mozambique. He served in southern Africa from 1972 to 1976.

From southern Africa, Bishop James was assigned to the Twelfth Episcopal District, which comprises Oklahoma and Arkansas. Bishop James continued his mission of excellence in Arkansas, where Shorter College received its accreditation and Bishop James became a close friend of Governor Bill Clinton, who is now the president of United States of America.

During this period, Bishop James became president of the Council of Bishops of the African Methodist Episcopal Church, serving in that office from 1982 to 1983. According to *Book of Discipline* of AME Church, the presidency of the Bishop's Council shall be for one year. In Arkansas, he built the human resource center at Shorter College and created an elderly handicapped project, Theressa James Manor, in North Little Rock.

In 1984, Bishop James was sent to his home District of South Carolina, where he had been born, reared and educated. Thus, he went back to the state which gave him his spiritual and intellectual foundation. Dr Coleman says that Bishop James transformed an uncertain future into great achievements. His coming to South Carolina was a process

The Theressa James Manor
Multi-family housing project for the elderly and handicapped,
North Little Rock, Arkansas

The F. C. James Human Resources Center
1980 AIA Design Award Winner
Shorter College
North Little Rock, Arkansas

Both of these projects were built by Bishop James when he
served as presiding Bishop of the Twelfth Episcopal District.
(Arkansas and Oklahoma, 1976-1984)

Bishop James and President Clinton, Hillary Rodham Clinton, and Dr. Theressa Gregg James

of "changing, creating, and innovating in the church." Bishop James believed that with God all good things were possible and his zeal made an impact on women's ministry, youth evangelism, theological and college education, history and economic development.

Bishop James put women in powerful, responsible positions thus acknowledging and accepting the great resource that God had bestowed on women. Many women under his bishopric became pastors and built churches.

Proverbs 22:6 tells us to train up the child in the way he or she should be and when he or she is old, he or she will not depart from it. Bishop James initiated the Youth Ministry in the District with emphasis on evangelism. Every two years Bishop James held a youth evangelistic extravaganza. The event featured young people preaching, testifying, singing and witnessing. The result of these extraordinary events were widespread youth conversions and commitments.

Bishop James was committed to improving the colleges and universities and to moving them toward accreditation. He reopened Dickerson Seminary on a full-time basis. He also established branches of the seminary in leading cities in the District to create greater access to theological education. He tirelessly promoted the college, encouraging local people to attend. Cognizant of the fact that many students needed financial assistance to attend college, Bishop James established a fund for theological education, leading Chaplain James A. Holmes, Jr., in the Bicentennial focus, to declare that, "Bishop James believed in a strong indigenous training program for the seventh Episcopal District Ministry."

Bishop James led Allen University to be accredited for the second time in its one-hundred ninety years of existence. In 1984, Bishop James had vowed that Allen University would rise again, and, indeed, it rose again.

Bishop James' entrepreneurial skills made him excel in economic development. He established the Seventh Episcopal District Economic Fund and raised over a quarter million dollars for Allen University endowment He also created a capital for Allen University which made capital accessible to businesses that could not get loans from banks and spurred new levels of black financial participation in South Carolina.

The Seventh Episcopal District achieved a new level of cooperation with the financial community under the leadership of Bishop James, which brought stronger banks to South Carolina and the nation.

Bishop James established the James Square Shopping Center, with the goal of leasing this multimillion dollar asset to increase the endowment of Allen University.

Bishop James also had a passion for history. He inspired Chaplain James A. Holmes, Sr. to write several manuscripts about the history of African Methodism in South Carolina. During the bicentennial year in 1987, Bishop James organized a group of scholars to write a 532-page hardcover book about African Methodism in South Carolina. The history of the AME church from 1787 to 1987 was documented with an emphasis on South Carolina. Much of the information in this book is drawn from that pioneering work.

Bishop James walks with kings and presidents but he has not lost touch with the ordinary man and woman. This is part of what has made him and his leadership great in the Seventh Episcopal District.

Though the bible teaches that a prophet is not honored in his own country, Bishop James has achieved wonders in his home state of South Carolina. Under his leadership the Seventh Episcopal District has seen:

- growth and expansion of the church;
- an expanded Reid Center for community service programs;
- laity newly inspired to contribute to Allen University's renaissance;
- the accreditation at Allen University;
- regular financial reports to all 7th District Constituency for the more than $7,000,000.00 in contributions;
- creation of new sanctuaries, educational buildings and parsonages;
- construction of housing for Hurricane Hugo victims through the AME 7th District/Habitat for Humanities Partnership
- an extended AME influence in government, ecumension, education, civic and corporate South Carolina, and many new programs, such as the Youth for Christ, the Debutante Showcase;
- a push on evangelism and membership as annual church priorities at annual conferences;

- strengthened and promoted programs of stewardship and tithing;
- re-established Social Action as the key church priority;
- organized a prayer service for peace in the Gulf War;
- promoted Christian Education;
- strengthened unity at the Seventh Episcopal District in working, planning and advancing together. *(Special Review)*

This ministry of Bishop James made presiding elders, ministers and lay persons urge the General Conference to return him to South Carolina for the second quadrennial.

In South Carolina F. C. James is known as:

F — Fidelity

C — Charismatic personality blended into and through South Carolina

J — Jet setter, chasing the coast and eradicatingdoubts that could not be done

A — Achiever, aiming high to succeed

M — Manager of the first magnitude with magnetic power pulling all forces together

E — Ever prevailing, ever pursuing to reach the goal

S — Servant of God, the community and country.

(Special Review on F. C. James)

Following his service in the Seventh District, Bishop James became Ecumenical Officer of the African Methodist Episcopal Church, representing the church on national and international ecumenical missions and ministry. His achievements in just one year were incredible and on August, 1993 the Bishops Council Office African Episcopal Church assigned Bishop James to the 2nd Episcopal District, which includes Maryland, Virginia, District of Columbia and North Carolina. He has become a great leader of the soaring 2nd District.

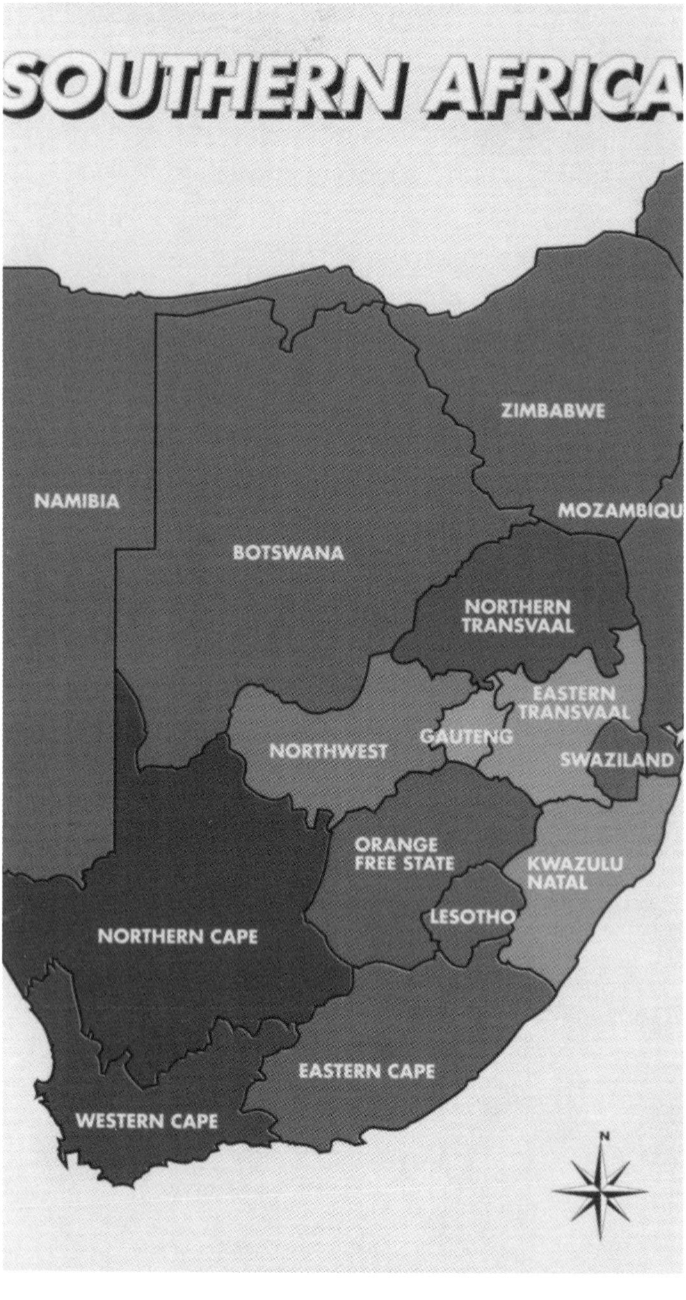
SOUTHERN AFRICA
ZIMBABWE
NAMIBIA
MOZAMBIQU
BOTSWANA
NORTHERN TRANSVAAL
EASTERN TRANSVAAL
GAUTENG
NORTHWEST
SWAZILAND
ORANGE FREE STATE
KWAZULU NATAL
LESOTHO
NORTHERN CAPE
EASTERN CAPE
WESTERN CAPE
N

6

A Missionary to Southern Africa

"Go ye therefore and teach all nations, baptizing them in the name of the Father, and of the Son and of the Holy Ghost."
MATTHEW 28:19 (KJV)

The African Methodist Episcopal Church has a tradition of sending the newly elected bishops overseas. Bishop James was sent to southern Africa from 1972 to 1976, where he presided over two districts, the Fifteenth Episcopal District and the Eighteenth Episcopal Church. These districts included six countries, Lesotho, Swaziland, Botswana, Mozambique, Namibia and South Africa.

Lesotho, Swaziland and Botswana were African countries, which were colonized by Britain. They later became British protectorates, and gained their independence from Britain in the 1960s. Although they were free countries, they depended on South Africa for their economic development. Lesotho and Swaziland still have strong traditional cultures with royal kings, King Moshoeshoe II of Lesotho and King Sobhuza of

Swaziland. Bishop James became a close friend of King Moshoeshoe II. He also became the Honorary Counsel-General of the kingdom of Lesotho in 1979 after his episcopal leadership in southern Africa.

Bishop James received his episcopal assignment in southern Africa just as Mozambique coming out of a civil war between Samora's Frelimo and the colonial Portuguese. Most of the country's whites left Mozambique for South Africa with their resources. Bishop James's challenge was to bring stability to the area. The United States did not have diplomatic relations with Mozambique's President Samora Machel because he espoused Marxist ideology in ruling the country.

Namibia was still called South West Africa. The country was first colonized by the Germans. After World War II, it fell under the administration of the League of Nations, and eventually South Africa was made its caretaker. During Bishop James' term the South West African People Organization, (SWAPO) was fighting against the South African Defense Forces to achieve the country's liberation. In South Africa, the doctrine of Apartheid was still entrenched. Blacks, colored, Indians and whites were legally separated and blacks and coloreds were not allowed to use white facilities.

The (mixed race) Coloreds and African belonged to the African Methodist Church, but though they were legally separated, Bishop James brought them together. He believed that in Christ there is not Jew or Gentile, man or woman, we all are one.

Politically southern Africa was oppressive, during his time;

however, Bishop James, a builder and developer, did great things.

In Cape Town, South Africa, which is the Fifteenth Episcopal District, he built the AME Publishing House. He understood that communication is the key to both the ministry and development. In South Africa, blacks were not allowed to dine in white hotels, but Bishop James had a church extravaganza at the downtown Holiday Inn in Cape Town, the first time in its history that this hotel allowed blacks to attend a function.

While in South Africa, Bishop James made friends with two rich black South Africans, Richard Moponya, who had a store in Soweto, and Ephraim Tshabalala, who owned the only cinema in Soweto. Bishop James solemnized Tshabalala's son's wedding to a Swazi princess. It was an extraordinary wedding.

In 1975, Bishop James built the James Multipurpose Center, with the auditorium that seated over 200 people and offices which the church rented to Family Planning of Lesotho and other businesses in Maseru, the capital of Lesotho.

Many new churches were built under Bishop James leadership. He encouraged education to his ministers in southern Africa and sent many of them to America to study, where they received master's degrees in Divinity from AME Schools and returned to rebuild the churches in southern Africa.

In 1973, Bishop founded a self-help African Methodist Episcopal ranch in Mbabane, the capital of Swaziland. In southern Africa, cattle are a mainstay of the economy. He

Fifteenth Episcopal District
and the
Eighteenth Episcopal District
of the
AFRICAN METHODIST EPISCOPAL CHURCH

THE RIGHT REVEREND F. C. JAMES, Presiding Bishop
1972 — 1976

THE AMEC* PRINTING AND PUBLISHING HOUSE**
BELLVILLE SOUTH CAPE PROVINCE, SOUTH AFRICA
DEDICATED DECEMBER, 1973

THE JAMES CENTRE OF AME SERVICE
MASERU, LESOTHO
DEDICATED APRIL, 1976

*African Methodist Episcopal Church
**Providing AME and Religious Literature to accomodate the linguistic needs and ethnic backgrounds of our Southern African constituency and their neighbors.

built James Chapel Church in Matsieng in Lesotho in the same year and organized the African Methodist Episcopal Network of Education in Maputo, the capital of Mozambique. He purchased the first AME property in Lobatse in Botswana and Bishop James built Hillside School in Manzini, one of the biggest towns in Swaziland, in 1974.

So it was not surprising that President Bill Clinton invited Bishop James to be a member of the official U.S. delegation to the inauguration of Nelson Mandela, the first black president of South Africa in May 1994. The delegation was led by Vice-President Al Gore and First Lady Hillary Rodham Clinton. It was a high honor for Bishop James to be present at the inauguration of a new day for South Africa, as he could recall vividly the oppressive apartheid government during his Episcopal leadership. On his way back to America, Bishop James was overjoyed and inspired and wrote this poem:

FLYING HOME FROM THE
NELSON MANDELA INAUGURATION

*Indelible images of South African liberation of the triumph
of Political righteousness in our time.
And before our eyes—and in our ears—and in our hearts—
and in our spirits: of Nelson Mandela—the Soaring symbol—the
Shining Son—the prepared personal—the People's preference
—the Able Advocate—The ANC Angel—
the Magnificent manifestation—the Momentous Man.*

*Dignity beyond dimension, Courage beyond contention, Readiness to
rule, smarts not learned in school, Support from strange sources,
facilitated from foreign Forces. Tears of joy and gladness, dilute
earlier thoughts of sadness. Victory yell singing from poorly housed*

peoples, Church bells ringing from Holy house steeples.
A moment in time with justice high—faulting,
When the leaders of the earth came bowing and saluting:
GREAT SOUTH AFRICA AT LAST IS FREE!
Now the American Delegation, sent by the Clinton administration,
Led by Vice-President and Mrs. Gore, First Lady, Hillary Clinton
and many more. Step about that star striped steel white bird,
Let the mighty jet engines under her wings be heard,
Lift her eagle-crested cabin toward the sky,
South Africa, we are leaving,
but we do not say, Goodbye.
—BISHOP FREDERICK C. JAMES, MAY, 1994

Mandela Inauguration, May, 1994

Bishop James never lost the ties he had in southern Africa. In November, 1994 he led about fifty African-American ministers and lay persons to southern Africa. It was the first time most of them had visited the area and Rev. Henry White said, "I will treasure forever my visit to southern Africa."

On January 3, 1996, Bishop and Mrs. James made their most recent trip to southern Africa to celebrate the 100 years of the African Methodist Episcopal Church in southern Africa. Bishop James's first stop was in Lesotho, where he visited his long-time friend King Moshoeshoe II. There he conducted a service at the palace with Basotho royalty on January 7, 1996, in Maseru. Two days later, on January 9th, King Moshoeshoe II was killed in an accident with his chauffeur. Though a great lost for Bishop James, there was a silver lining. Bishop James was able to have a worship with the king, and minister to him, two days before he died, a blessing only God could have made possible. The bishop was at least able to see his friend for the last time. While in southern Africa, Bishop also visited (Maseru), Lesotho, (Bulawayo) Zimbabwe, (Windhoek) Namibia, (Cape Town, Bloemfontein and Johannesburg, Soweto) South Africa and (Mbabane) Swaziland.

Bishop James preached a centennial sermon in the 19th Episcopal District at Vista University Auditorium in Soweto. The auditorium seats about 5,000 people. In his sermon Bishop included Sesotho and Zulu words. After the sermon 46 were converted.

THE AFRICAN METHODIST EPISCOPAL CHURCH
CENTENNIAL SERMON

The Faith Upon Which We Stand
Delivered at Vista University-Soweto, Johannesburg
Text: Hebrews 11:1-2
"Now faith is the substance of things hoped for, the evidence of things not seen. For by faith, the Elders obtained a good report."

Salutation:

Bishop John H. Adams, Bishop H.B. Senatle, Bishop F.H. Talbot, Bishop Donald G. Ming, Bishop Robert Thomas, Bishop McKinley Young and Bishop R.V. Webster, Bishops' Spouses, General Connectional Officers, College Presidents, Deans, WMS President, Lay Organization President Williams, District Leadership Officers, Presiding Elders, Pastors, Laity; Revered Ecumenical Associates, Distinguished Officials of State, Region, and Community, Brothers and Sisters in the Lord and those who ought to be, in the Mighty Name of Jesus, we greet you at this time.

Thank you Bishop Cousin for reminding me one more time of the man I'd like to be. Believe me I shall continue to try to be somebody who tried to do some good somewhere. I want to thank Bishop H.B. Senatle for inviting me to deliver The Centennial Sermon today.

We, Mrs. James and I had the honor, privilege and good fortune to serve for Four (4) years in this area, the Districts which are now the 15th, 18th and 19th. The relationship which we formed as we worked together here will be with us for the rest of our lives.

In May, 1994, I was honored by the President of The United States, Bill Clinton to Represent The United States of America as one of 44 Designees led by Vice President Gore and Mrs. Clinton at The Presidential Inauguration of His Excellency Nelson Mandela.

Having served for Four (4) Years in apartheid South Africa, the ecstasy of the moment of Inauguration will be forever etched in my memory. He knows of my love for southern Africa and his kindness has me standing here today. I solicit your prayers to God that I may do his will in this place behind this pulpit here today.

"What Mean These Stones"

Some travelers were traveling through the Everglades of Florida in the United States of America and they began to encounter little mounds of stones along the journey... One mound of stones at one place and then after a while...another.

Finally, overcome with curiosity, the leader of the traveling party asked the question— *"What Mean These Stones?"*

They said, "There is a 100 year old native among us, ask him." They asked him, *"What Mean These Stones?"* He, said, "These stones are here as indicators that there are Alligators in the area."

"Look down and then look up!"

For One Hundred Years (100) scattered across the surface of southern Africa there are Hundreds of Cornerstones that say A.M.E. Church.

They are also there because there are Alligators in the area.

There are Alligators of Powerlessness—Alligators of Poverty

There are Alligators of Infidelity—and Alligators of Immorality

"THE FAITH UPON WHICH WE STAND"

There are Alligators of Ignorance—and Alligators of Sin

There are Alligators of Helplessness—and Alligators of Guilt

There are Alligators of Hopelessness—and Alligators of Doubt

For One Hundred (100) Years in southern Africa A.M.E. Cornerstones have said "Look Down and then Look Up!!"

To God Be The Glory, Great Things He Has Done....

Praise The Lord; Praise The Lord, Let The Earth Hear His Voice:

Let The People Rejoice

O Come To The Father, through Jesus the Son, and give Him the glory great things He has done.

From the Mountain—Crested Kingdom of Lesotho,to the Water—soaked Flatlands of Zimbabwe;

From the Diamond—Rich hills of Namibia to the

Picturesque areas of Capetown (South Africa);

From the Lush Green Expanses of Swaziland, to the

History impacted Church Land of Pretoria;

From the Golden Glowing Streets of Johannesburg, to our

Sisters and our Brothers of Soweto.

We have come to Celebrate One Hundred (100) Years.

We have been showered by the hospitality of our host

Bishops and by the Splendid Spouses who walk by their side.

We have been inspired by the Dedication of our Church in South Africa. We have been hypnotized by the Singing that identifies the Region. We have been energized by the Stewardship that's so much greater than our own. We have come to Celebrate One Hundred (100) Years. We have dined and we have danced and we have made sure of this Chance. To make our African Sisters and Brothers know we care.

"THE FAITH UPON WHICH WE STAND"

We have come to rejoice with you and to salute your progress too.

But most of all to make you know—We're standing near!

We have come to hear the Story; and to give to God the Glory

We have come to see our Members in their Land

We have come to share our Stewardship

And to acknowledge our Savior's Lordship

And to affirm our African Kinship as we Stand!

TO GOD BE THE GLORY

For the A.M.E. Story

In southern most Africa

Is a part of His Plan!

Therefore, The Centennial Message today is a message about

Faith—

The Faith of 100 Years —It was Mighty Faith a Saving Faith.

A Faith that did not shrink

Though pressed by every foe

That did not tremble on the brink of any earthly woe.

That did not Murmur nor complain

beneath the Chastening rod

It leaned upon its God.

It was a faith resigned, submissive, meek

Believing pure and clean

Where only Christ is heard to speak

His Spirit deep within

You Prayed

Lord, give us such a faith as this

And then whatever may come

We'll taste even here the hallowed bliss

of our eternal home.

"THE FAITH UPON WHICH WE STAND"

Come now, and draw a little nearer, let's look a little closer at this Faith that has lasted 100 Years.

Surely, during the last 100 Years in southern Africa

We have seen The Lightning Flashing

We have heard The Thunder Roll

We have seen High Waves a'dashing

Trying to conquer our Soul

But we have heard the voice from the Captain

Saying "My Sailor — Hold on!"

He promised never to leave us — never to leave us alone!

WHAT IS THE FIRST STEP OF THE FAITH THAT LASTS ONE HUNDRED (100) YEARS?

IT IS...

"THE FAITH UPON WHICH WE STAND"

I. (IT IS) A BELIEF IN GOD OUR FATHER MODIMO NTATE WA RONA

    It is a basic belief in a Mighty God who relates to us as Father.

A. It is knowing that the God that we trust is OMNIPOTENT

    It is knowing that the God that we serve is ABLE

    It is knowing that the God that we serve is READY

It is knowing that the God that we serve is WILLING

The Hymnist: Say O Lord our God, When in Awesome Wonder

Consider all the Worlds thy hands have made

I see the stars — I hear the rolling Thunder

Thy Power throughout The Universe display

Then Sings my Soul my Savior God to Thee

How great Thou Art — How great Thou Art

Modimo Ntate — God our Father, God our Father

"THE FAITH UPON WHICH WE STAND"

B. It is knowing that The God that we trust is OMNISCIENT

That He sees all I do; That He hears all I say; A God who is writing all the time.

"Why should I feel discouraged"

Why should the shadows come

Why should my heart be lonely

And long for heaven and home

When Jesus is my Captain

My constant friend is He

His eye is on the Sparrow

And I know he watches me,

And I know he watches me

So I sing because I'm happy

I sing because I'm free

For His eye is on the Sparrow

And I know He watches me—Modimo Ntate

God our Father

FOR 100 YEARS WE HAVE STOOD

II. (WE STAND) ON THE BELIEF OF CHRIST OUR REDEEMER

    Kreste Mopholosi Wa Rona (SESOTHO)

    Umisindisi Wami (SEZULU)

    Not Jesus — A Great Prophet— But Kreste Mopholosi

    Not Jesus — A Great Spirit— But Kreste Mopholosi

    Not Jesus — A Great Man— But Kreste Mopholosi

    In Adam we all died; But in Christ we were made Alive

    Our souls were in hock at the Devils Pawnshop

    Then Jesus came — In The Fullness of Time

    was born of Mary in Bethlehem.

    The Angels sang over Shepherds' Field.

    Joy To The World, The Lord is Come

Let Earth Receive her King

Let Every Heart Prepare Him Room

And Heaven and Nature Sing

"Go Tell It On The Mountain

Over The Hills and Everywhere

Go Tell It On The Mountain

That Jesus Christ is Born"

And then in the fullness of time, our Redemption drew nigh.

They nailed Him to a Cross on a hill called Calvary

Isaiah had already said "Surely He Has Borne our Griefs and Carried Our Sorrows; Yet we did esteem Him stricken, Smitten of God and Afflicted. But He was wounded for our transgressions: He was bruised for our iniquities. The chastment of our peace was upon him. But early Sunday morning, He got up; He got up.

For 100 Years We Have Stood On

III. A BELIEF IN MAN OUR BROTHER-INDODANA WETHU

Motho Morena (Sesotho) Indoda Nawethun/Bhuti (Sezulu)

Mang Kapa Mang Ke o Buti

"We believe that God is no respecter of persons"

In spite of Ethnic Conflict, We believe Motho Morena

In the midst of persecution, We believe Motho Morena

Under the burden of Apartheid, We believe Motho Morena

Even after the Sharpeville Slaughter, We believe Motho Morena

After the 1976 Shooting of The Children, We believe Motho Morena

We believe in Man Our Brother.

"The Average Man is the man of the mill

The Man of the Valley, the man of the hill

The Man at the throttle, the man at the Plow

The Man with the fruit of his toil on his brow

Who brings into being the dreams of the few

Who works for himself, for me, and for you

There is not a purpose, a project, or plan

But rests on the strength of the toil of his hand

The growth of a City — might of a Land.

Closing:

FINALLY, WE ARE HERE AFTER ONE HUNDRED (100)

YEARS OF TESTIMONY

The Testimony of Word and Deed.

The Apostle Paul, The Hebrew Zealot turned Christian on

The Road to Damascus, wrote a letter to his fellow Hebrews.

In this letter, he said

"Now faith is the substance of things hoped for, the evidence of things not seen. For by faith, the Elders obtained a good report." Hebrews 11:1—2

As an African American at an African Centennial, I want to call the names of some Elders who hoped for some things and didn't see others, but they also made a good report during the past One Hundred (100) Years.

Well, the Church itself is built on Testimony.

On the Coast of Caesarean Phillippi, Jesus conducted an Opinion Poll among His Disciples one day "The question was "Whom do men say that I the Son of Man am?"

It was an Opinion Poll!

Jesus knew who God, His Father said He was!

His Father had said, "This my beloved Son in Whom I am well pleased."

Jesus Knew Who The Prophets said He was!

The Prophets had said, "He shall be called IMMANUEL,

WONDERFUL, COUNSELOR, MIGHTY GOD, PRINCE OF PEACE."

Jesus Knew Who He Himself Said He Was!

He had said, I AM The Good Shepherd, I Am The True Vine, I Am The Door, I Am The Way, I Am The Truth, I Am The Light.

But Who do Men say that I Am? They said:

Some say you're John The Baptist, Some Elias

Others Jeremiahs or one of the Prophets

Jesus then asked, "Who do you say that I am?"

Simon Peter answered with Personal Testimony, He said to me

"THOU ART THE CHRIST, THE SON OF THE LIVING GOD!"

Jesus said to Simon, "Blessed are THOU Simon Barjona. Flesh and blood hath not revealed this unto Thee, But my Father which is in Heaven. I am going to change your name

"THOU art Peter and upon this rock, I will build my Church and the Gates of Hell shall not prevail against it."

Jesus Knew who He was, but what He needed was a Witness who would Testify by Faith. The Disciples all had titles, but Peter had a Testimony. And upon the Rock of Peter's Testimony, Christ build a Church.

Rock—Bottomed

Custom Built and Shock Proof

What about the next One Hundred (100) Years

It depends upon our Testimony.

I don't know about you, but,

"I was sinking deep in Sin

Far from the peaceful shore

very deeply stained within

Sinking to rise no more, but the Master of the sea, heard my despairing cry, From the altars lifted me, now safe am I.

Love lifted me, Love lifted, when nothing else could help, Love lifted me.

For the next hundred years in southern Africa our Testimonies will continue to be God the Father, Modima Ntate, Christ our Redeemer, Kreste Mopholosi, Man our brother, Motho Morena, The Faith upon which we stand. For the next hundred years we are going to lift Him Up! Lift Him Up, Lift the precious Savior up, because He said "If I be lifted up from the earth, I will draw all men unto me. The Faith upon which we stand, the Faith upon which we stand for the next hundred years. Amen.

In Sesotho we say, "Rea leboha ntate, Bishop James. Mosebetsi wa hao a motle lefatseng la rona. Le ka moso, modimo a ho hlohonolofatse. Thank you for your works, Bishop James, in our homeland. May God bless you.

7

A Soldier for Justice

*"The Spirit of the Lord is upon me...
to liberate the oppressed."*
LUKE 4:18-19 (TEV)

The ministry of Bishop James was not only spiritual, but included the needs of the whole person: the mind, the physical needs, social and political needs. He was at Mt. Pisgah when he developed his political activism. In 1960 he authored the "Social Action Bill for the AME Church. This bill led to the development of the AME Commission on Social Action. Bishop James was elected its first director and joined the General Board.

According to the AME's *Book of Discipline*, the duties of the Commission on Social Action shall be to conduct studies, make pronouncements and issue directives embracing Christian issues. It assists in the direction of African Methodist Christian Social witness in all matters relating to home, relations and Christian citizenship.

At the bishopric level, the presiding Bishop appoints members of the Social Action Committee who report to the annual conference.

Also according to the AME's *Book of Discipline*, a part time consultant is elected to coordinate the Social Action Commission at the Connectional level and he/she is the member of the General Board. Bishop James became a pioneer of social activism in the AME Church.

In 1966 he was appointed a delegate to the world conference of Church and Society in Geneva, Switzerland. The goal of the conference was to involve the church in social and political issues.

Bishop James joined the National Association for the Advancement of the Colored People in order to participate in the civil rights movements, moving in the Spirit of the Lord, to preach good news to the poor, open the eyes of the blind, release prisoners, and liberate the oppressed. He was president of the NAACP Sumter branch from 1965 to 1972. He became a lifetime member of NAACP in 1968 and during his term as branch President he was instrumental in the desegregation of the city of Sumter. He was arrested twice during the civil rights movement. First after the bombing of a church in Montgomery, and second on August 1, 1963 when marchers demonstrated against a white hotel.

His civil rights leadership in South Carolina made him a well known trusted figure among several governors of South Carolina. He was a board member of the South Carolina Congressional District Caucus and a member of the South Carolina Democratic Party. Through his political activism and

Bishop James leading a 1960's Civil Rights March in Sumter, South Carolina

civil rights campaigns and his leadership in the church he was invited to the White House by four American presidents, John F. Kennedy, Lyndon B. Johnson, Jimmy Carter and Bill Clinton.

In 1989, he became co-chairman of the South Carolina Legislative Black Caucus. He was involved with its reapportionment committee and in the same year was appointed to the Select Committee of the Richmond County Administrative Building Site. The governor of South Carolina also appointed him to the Governor's Commission on Economic Recovery of South Carolina.

Bishop James was also involved in social issues such as Alcohol—Drug Abuse, Elderly-Handicapped Project Housing and the environment. In 1987 the governor appointed him to the Governor's Strategic Council on Drug Education, Enforcement and Treatment and to the Greater Columbia Convention Center Site Committee. He was elected vice chairman of the Columbia Housing Authority and also became member of the Advisory Council Board of Habitat for Humanity, an organization involved with the environment in 1988. He became a Trustee Board member of the Palmetto Partnership, a state foundation for drug abuse prevention. As the Apostle Paul had a talent for making tents, Bishop James had a entrepreneurial talent, which he used in the church to profit families and communities.

The development of James Square, a shopping center in Columbia, South Carolina, attests to his gift of taking small things and building them.

In 1991, Bishop James was elected to the Board of the National Bank of South Carolina. He was also a board member of the Urban League, and vice-chairman of its service and development agency. Other service organizations Bishop James pledged were, shriner in Cairo Temple No. 125 of Columbia, South Carolina, 330 Mason of Prince Hall C.C. Johnson Consistory number 136 and a member of St.Paul Lodge No. 8 in Sumter, South Carolina. He was on the various boards to make an impact in decision making to benefit the community and the church.

Rev. Mammie Williams, pastor of Hughes Memorial United Methodist Episcopal Church in Washington, D.C. recalls the impact of Bishop James in civil rights issues:

> As a youth growing up in Sumter, South Carolina, Bishop James and Mrs. James were very special black leaders during the early 60's. It was at Mt. Pisgah AME Church that our NAACP chapter thrived with the development of young black leadership. Bishop James and Mrs. James were visionaries and staunch civil rights advocates. They were on the front lines and yet ever present to counsel with youth. They, along with several Baptists, United Methodist pastors in Sumter planted and nurtured the seeds for my own understanding of religion without actions is a dead religion and is due a rightful burial. It was there at Mt. Pisgah that laity and clergy plotted and planned the sit-ins and marches that helped to change the course of history in Sumter and in the South Carolina.
>
> Therefore, it was no real surprise to me when they were elected to the episcopacy and then assigned to southern Africa. They are faithful servants. All that the Jameses have contributed to the church of Jesus Christ and kingdom building on earth is good. To God be the glory!

Rev. Jesse Jackson at the 1996 Founders Week Celebration at Ebenezer Fort Washington states:

> Bishop James is my confidant. He is a counter-culture Bishop, with a holistic gospel. He used prayer and votes together in the church. He brought honor to our church. He lives the life he preaches about. He has honor, intellect and spirituality.

8

Ecumenical Influence

"One Lord, one faith, one baptism"
EPHESIANS 4:5 (KJV)

In 1992, Bishop James became the ecumenical officer of the general conference of African Methodist Episcopal Church, national and international.

The Ecumenical officer represents the African Methodist Episcopal Church in ecumenical organizations such as to the National Council of Churches of Christ and the World Council of Churches and also promotes ecumenical dialogue with other denominations. Bishop James became the member of the governing board of the National Council of Churches of Christ in New York. In 1966, before his appointment to the ecumenical office, he served as delegate to the World Council of Churches and also as delegate to the World Federation of Methodism.

Through his participation in the National Council of Churches of Christ, Bishop James was instrumental in involving the African Methodist Episcopal Church in the ministry of eco-justice. The interfaith, multi-racial education and action initiative to address issues of environmental health risk from hazardous and toxic waste sites in North Carolina and southeastern Virginia helped the church protect the sacredness of humanity, provide interfaith doctrinal and theological support to theocentric, eco-centric and prophetic justice perspectives.

The United Church of Christ and the U.S. government Accounting Office reported that of the more than 80.5 million pounds of toxic pollutants released annually into North Carolina's air, water and soil, a disproportionately high percentage affects the African-American and Native American communities. Bishop James endorsed the economic justice ministry to educate the community about pollutants in the environment and secured funds from the National Council of Churches of Christ for eco-justice ministry in the AME church.

At the 1995 annual conferences, Rev. Solomon T. Holley and Rev. Dr. Mankekolo Mahlangu-Ngcobo, the present writer, addressed members about the necessity to save God's earth, which is our home. Material resources for congregational study were distributed to every pastor.

9

Healing the Second Episcopal District

"With His stripes we are healed."
ISAIAH 53:5 (KJV)

On Monday November 1, 1993, a bus left Metropolitan AME Church in Washington at about 7 a.m. for Philadelphia, Pennsylvania. We sang and prayed to God for a healer to the Second District. We joined riders from other cities in the Second Episcopal District in Philadelphia at 9 a.m. There were some visitors from other Episcopal districts. The meeting was held at the headquarters of the First Episcopal District. We were about five hundred. Retired Presiding Elder, Rev. Walter Hildebrand presided at the meeting and explained the AME polity concerning reassignment of bishops.

Rev. I.W. Knight, Pastor of St. John AME in Norfolk, Virginia said, "At the time, we were a constituency in need of a leader sent by God. We were in need of an Episcopal leader with special skills, anointing, creativity, a Christian leader, a preacher, an educator, negotiator, businessman, and financier, a reconciliator, someone to bring peace, a pastor loving, enabler to help in ministry and economic development to give us encouragement and restoration, a national leader, a prophet of the Second Episcopal District. The one who will make us return to basics."

The Council of Bishops, is the executive branch of the Connectional African Methodist Episcopal Church, which meets annually in between the quadrennial general conference. The council met in the board room. There were periods of tension and prayer. The group broke for lunch and afterward was told that the bishops were ready announce who would be the next Bishop of the Second Episcopal District. The bishops entered the auditorium, led by the President of the Bishop Council, Bishop John Richard Bryant, who reported that after prayer and discussions, the council had selected Bishop Frederick Calhoun James of the African Methodist Episcopal church. Rev. Dr. William P. DeVeaux stood and thanked the Bishop for assigning a new bishop, welcomed Bishop James, and promised to work through the spirit of God to provide unity and healing in the District. There was prayer and the meeting adjourned.

Bishop James' and Mother Theressa Gregg James became officially our leaders. His first challenge was to unite and heal the ministers and lay persons in the district. He treated everyone the same, having neither favorites or a clique. He was straight forward. If he does not like a thing, he says it loud and clearly and corrects it in order to move forward. His meetings, at District planning, founders week and annual conferences are operated professionally and efficiently.

His ordination services are spiritual, In 1994 during his first annual conference, he ordained ministers and deacons and ordained as Elders. Rev. Sherita G. Seawright and the present writer. The spiritual experience was phenomenal.

His mission in the Second Episcopal Church was not only to be a pastor to pastors but also to address legal and financial challenges. He knew the best lawyers in Washington and he did an excellent job. At the Founders Week celebration he invited one to give the membership the legal report. The Bishop earned respect for his candor, which allowed everyone in the church to be informed about church business.

The financial challenges were enormous. Bishop James asked the church to give money, and led by example. When he took the challenge to serve the Second District, the church was in the red, In his second year as Bishop, it had balanced its budget and had a surplus.

Here are testimonies of ministers and lay persons in the Second District about the impact of his leadership.

> *Bishop James is a blessing to the Second Episcopal District and the whole A.M.E. Church. He is a Christian, a deep spiritual thinker, a master of the church history and a man of personal stewardship to God and humankind. He has encouraged voting registration, and has done God's work on earth. He has encouraged pastors to go out and bring people to church and to the Lord. Bishop James is a kind, spiritual family man who continues to embrace economic empowerment and enhancement of the quality of life among the people. He loves the A.M.E. church and he loves almighty God.*
>
> REV. GEORGE A. MANNING, PRESIDING ELDER
> POTOMAC DISTRICT, WASHINGTON CONFERENCE

Bishop James has done a tremendous work in the Second Episcopal District. He was able to cover both the religious and political arena, something not usually done. Economically he worked with other churches on problems of faith. He worked with President Bill Clinton on America's relationship with Africa. He brought traditionalism, a new sense of African Methodism, enthusiasm, healing and reconciliation. The District has grown numerically. He alleviated the debt and saved the District money. As a Senior Bishop, he has been able to solve all the problems of the District with wisdom.

REV. GOODWIN DOUGLASS, PRESIDING ELDER
CAPITAL DISTRICT, WASHINGTON CONFERENCE

Bishop James stabilized the District. People began to talk to each other. Communication was open in difficult situations. It is a miracle of unity through strong leadership and faith. He made the District second to none, a district whose achievements all admire.

REV. E.O. SAUNDERS, PRESIDING ELDER
NORTHERN DISTRICT, NORTH CAROLINA CONFERENCE

Bishop James' impact in the Second District stemmed from his presence among all his constituency, laity and clergy. He is a man of compassionate heart and wisdom, who flies above the storm and leads others in doing the same.

REV. E.C. HUMPHREY, PRESIDING ELDER
SOUTHERN DISTRICT, NORTH CAROLINA CONFERENCE

Bishop James is a great leader, an effective preacher and an outstanding administrator.

REV. W. PAGE, PRESIDING ELDER
NORFOLK, PORTSMOUTH DISTRICT, VIRGINIA CONFERENCE

Bishop James is a profound leader, called of God, a developer of people, a caring bishop.

REV. PAUL CLIFFORD ADKINS, PRESIDING ELDER
RICHMOND ROANOKE DISTRICT, VIRGINIA CONFERENCE

Bishop James brought togetherness, a spirit of harmony and friendliness. He lifted the spirit of Second Episcopal District to make us aware of our duties as AME's. The main thought is that he brought us to the basis of African Methodism.

REV. E.C. WILSON, PRESIDING ELDER
EASTERN DISTRICT, BALTIMORE CONFERENCE

Bishop James has had a tremendous impact on the Second Episcopal District since his arrival. He has been a bishop who has given of his leadership equally to all people. He came into a situation of great crisis. Due to his stability and godliness he was able in a short period of time to restore the Second Episcopal District to one of solidarity and cohesiveness.

REV. EARLE BROOKS, PRESIDING ELDER
BALTIMORE DISTRICT, BALTIMORE CONFERENCE

Bishop James gave fresh leadership to us all in striving for greater heights. He is accountable. He encourages us to save souls and be Christian men and women, leaders in the community and at home.

REV. J.R. CROUTCHFIELD, PRESIDING ELDER
WESTERN DISTRICT, NORTH CAROLINA CONFERENCE

Bishop James has done a marvelous job in the Second District. He brought financial and spiritual healing.

REV. TYSON COLEMAN, PRESIDING ELDER
EASTERN DISTRICT, NORTH CAROLINA CONFERENCE

Bishop James has compassion, love, and he is trying to bring about peace in the District. He stabilized the District and his appointments have been well thought out and have met the needs of the people. He works in a team spirit with Mrs. James, who is firm and disciplined beside him. He was able to solve problems without alarming people.

MR. JOSEPH COLUMBUS MCKINNEY, TREASURER OF THE AFRICAN METHODIST EPISCOPAL CHURCH, GENERAL BOARD MEMBER

The Second Episcopal District was in need of his financial acumen and experience in church and civic life just at the time he came. He was God ordained and appointed. The impact Bishop James made in a short time from November 3, 1993 was to eliminate a large, vast amount of debts the District had incurred in such a way that it should not be a burden to the people of God. He has created peace and comraderie in the District.

He initiated new appointments as they relate to Ministry Beyond the Sanctuary, a vision way before his time. He has made the AME church have impact beyond the church walls.

He has reestablished the unquestionable leadership in Washington which has contact with the White House and the Ecumenical movement in Washington.

He has made the Second Episcopal District headquarters a place of advice and counsel for churches, Congress and the executive branch of government. The AME church in the Second Episcopal District has restored respectability.

He exposed the District to other parts of the world. He had two trips to southern Africa and one to Caribbean. He has endured the hardships silently as he was trying to solve his problems. He is a fair bishop who treats every preacher, whether from a mega church or a small church, the same.

In a short time, the Second Episcopal Church is soaring.

Rev. W.W. Easley, Jr., Treasurer Second Episcopal District
Pastor of Campbell A.M.E. Church, Washington, D.C.

Bishop James came to the Second District when it labored under an atmosphere of fear, distrust, suspicion and anger. The District was divided and wounded. He brought skillful administration, impeccable integrity, unwavering commitment, superb financial management, strong and visionary leadership. These skills were combined to heal the wounds of the District, repair its financial brokenness of the District, and restore a sense of pride to members.

His reputation, his association with President Clinton, as well as kings and international dignitaries, and his honorable character have positively impacted on the office of the bishop.

Rev. Conrad Bridges, Pastor
Greater Bethel AME Church, Charlotte, North Carolina

He made us return to basics in the AME tradition. His commitment to social change through voter registration, political activism and economic development have had a great impact on the Second Episcopal District.

Rev. Edgar James, Pastor
Turner Memorial AME Church, Washington, D.C.

Bishop James is a man of truth, tradition and talent. He exemplifies the best of the AME church. He is a bishop ahead of his time and a man for all seasons.

Rev. William Wingo, Pastor
Mt. Zoare AME Church, Baltimore, Maryland

Bishop James is a great teacher of African Methodism and empowerment. He has brought unity to the Second Episcopal District. I praise the Lord for his leadership.

REV. BEATRICE C. EDWARDS, PASTOR
MT. SINAI AME CHURCH, LAPLATA, MARYLAND

He brought unity, healing, reconciliation and sound financial management.

REV. HARRY C. SEAWRIGHT, PASTOR
UNION BETHEL AME CHURCH, BRANDYWINE, MARYLAND

Bishop James has pursued excellence in his ministry. He encouraged the use of AME hymnals in worship. He has empathy for those who suffer. His sermons focus on faith, fellowship, family and franchise. His work is a constant reminder that we are sons and daughters of Allen. More women pastors have been delegates and alternates to the General Conference under his leadership.

REV. VIVIAN B. CASTAIN, PASTOR
STEVENSON AME CHURCH, BALTIMORE, MARYLAND

Bishop James is spiritual, inspirational, and his increased atmosphere of fellowship among us. He has been a healing balm to a wounded and aching District. A good product of South Carolina.

REV. JOHN W. DUCKETTE, PASTOR
GRACE AME CHURCH, CATONSVILLE, MARYLAND

Bishop James has been a catalyst for healing and reconciliation. He has been a father figure concerned about our youth and their education.

REV. THOMAS JONES, PASTOR
FAMILY RELATIONS - MINISTRY BEYOND THE SANCTUARY

Bishop James has had a great impact on healing resentments and anger and through his financial management. His economic development system has saved money. His vision of ministry Beyond The Sanctuary has helped other ministers to use their skills and talents to the fullest.

DR. IRIS KEYS, ASSISTANT MINISTER
ALLEN AME CHURCH, BALTIMORE, MARYLAND

He is a healer, visionary for the Second Episcopal Church. A businessman, a preacher, a model Christian and a Bishop who personifies the creed: God our Father, Christ our redeemer, man our brother. He emulates the work of the Founder, Richard Allen, through economic development, self-empowerment and proclaiming the good News.

REV. HENRY WHITE, PASTOR
BROWN MEMORIAL AME CHURCH, WASHINGTON, D.C.

Bishop James with Vice President Al Gore and Mrs. James

10

The Ministry Beyond the Sanctuary

"And there are diversities of operations but in the same God which worketh all in all."
I CORINTHIANS 12:6 (KJV)

Sunday church service aims to evangelize and inspire worshipers who come with burdens, sadness, sickness, disappointments, and hurt. The preacher exalts the name of the Lord, the choir is singing and prayers are said. Usually it takes one and a half to two hours to complete the spiritual celebrations. Then the question comes, "What happens after the Sunday morning worship? What is going to happen beyond the sanctuary on Monday, Tuesday, Wednesday, Thursday, Friday and Saturday? What about those who are unable to come to the service? And what happens to ministers who are called by God to the ministry, not necessarily to be pastors of churches?" Bishop James wrestled with these questions and evolved the idea of a Ministry Beyond the Sanctuary. Most of the ministry of Jesus was done beyond the sanctuary. Jesus preached, taught and healed on the mountains, on the roads, by the sea, from city to city, and in homes.

Bishop James had the vision of ministers reaching out to the homeless, to those in prisons, and to young and old alike. He brought ministry to university and community college students, to families, to urban youth groups, to nursing homes; to black men and women, to youth at risk, to substance abusers, to the emotionally ill, and to government officials. In all, Bishop James developed 63 ministries beyond the sanctuary in the Second Episcopal District. At every annual conference the pastors give reports on their ministries. Lives have been changed in prisons, nursing homes, college campuses and hospitals.

In assessing the impact of Bishop James in the Second District, Rev. Ann Lighter Fuller, Pastor of Mt. Calvary AME Church in Towson, Maryland, said that the primary achievement in the District is the Creation of the Ministry Beyond the Sanctuary. Our church places too much emphasis on the pastoral ministry. There is an army of capable ministers who may not have the opportunity or feel the calling to be a pastor, yet who have other gifts that can be used for the Glory of God. The Ministry Beyond the Sanctuary has allowed many of these gifted and talented ministers to help others.

The following is a list of the historic ministries beyond the sanctuary, their pastors, and where these ministries are based.

Prison Ministry
REV. ABRAHAM SMITH, JR.
MONTGOMERY COUNTY DETENTION CENTER

REV. EUGENE RADCLIFF
CHARLES COUNTY PRISON

Rev. Shirley M. Anderson
Jessup Women's Prison

Rev. Evelyn L. Horne
Prison After Care Ministry

Rev. Barbara Ridley
Ministry Correctional Resources

Rev. Herman Gladney
Prince William County Detention Facility

Rev. Deborah Wright
Eastern Correctional Institution

Rev. Josephine Hill
Juvenile Services Ministry, Baltimore Detention Center

Rev. Pearl Jeter
Women's Prison Ministry-Baltimore and Jessup, Maryland

Rev. Kenneth Dunn
MD Youth Detention Center-Washington

Rev. Jymn Turner, Jr.
Juvenile Correction Ministry-Virginia

Campus Ministry
Rev. Marlene D. Sumes
Gallaudet University

Rev. Gayle A. Perkins
Prince George's Community College

Rev. Constance C. Wheeler
Howard University

Rev. Brenda White
University of Maryland-Baltimore

Rev. Rashid Pinckney
Morgan State University-Baltimore

Rev. Perdite Johnson
Southeast Washington

Rev. Florida Morehead
Ministry to College Students-Washington

Rev. Rebecca R. Rivka
Norfolk State University

Rev. Shelton Sullivan
Bowie State University

Hospital Chaplaincy

Rev. Patricia A. Swann
Children's Hospital

Rev. Franklin Thomas
National Rehabilitation Center

Rev. Etoria Goggins
Howard University Hospital

Rev. LaTonya Sullivan
Doctor's Hospital

Rev. Izear Tyous
Greater South East Hospital

Rev. Dorothy Gross
Hospital Chaplain Ministry-Baltimore

Rev. Ronald Ferguson
Southern Maryland Hospital

Rev. Kathy O. Berkley
Wake County-Raleigh

Rev. Claudette. V. Delpino,
Wake County

Rev. Linda Singletary
Orange County-Charlotte

Nursing Home Ministry
Rev. Betty M. Smith
Hyattsville Manor

Rev. Marvin Glenn
Greater S.E. Senior Citizens Home

Rev. Dianne D. Coles
Washington Nursing Home, Washington, D.C.

Rev. Brenda McClain
Golden Oaks, Laurel

Rev. Pauline Thurston
Rolling Crest Nursing Home Commons Ministry

Rev. Barbara D. Crawford
Mecklenburg City-Charlotte

Hospice Ministry
Rev. Frances Sparkman
Union Bethel-Randallstown

Rev. Catherine Ferguson
Trinity Hospice Ministry

Pastoral Counseling
Rev. Michelle Balamani
Washington Conference

Rev. Angela Wainwright
Pastoral Care and Counseling

Rev. Teresa Lawrence
Pastoral Care/Family Counseling, North Carolina-Southern District

Eco-Justice
Rev. Dr. Mankekolo Mahlangu-Ngcobo
Washington Conference

Ministry to Youth
REV. KELLIE V. HAYES
NEW LIBERATION A.M.E. CHURCH

REV. RICHARD GREEN
PARKVILLE HIGH SCHOOL

REV. GEORGE RICE
SAMUEL GOMPERS ELEMENTARY SCHOOL

REV. BRENDA CARTER
BOOKER T. WASHINGTON HIGH SCHOOL

Family Relations Ministry
REV. PHYLLIS R. RAMSEY
EBENEZER (FT. WASHINGTON)

Ministry to the Christian Entrepreneur
REV. DIANNE JOHNSON
EBENEZER (FT. WASHINGTON)

Homeless Ministry
REV. SHERITA G. SEAWRIGHT
PRINCE GEORGE'S HYATTSVILLE

REV. GWENDOLYN I. DUFFY
WESLEY HEIGHTS AREA-CHARLOTTE

MR. HARRY SIMPSON
SHELTER/HOMELESS-WESTERN NORTH CAROLINA, RALEIGH, NC

It is our prayer that Bishop James' vision of the ministry beyond the century will spread throughout the AME Episcopal districts as he retires in July, 1996, at the General Conference in Louisville, Kentucky.

On Friday, February 9, 1996 at the closing of 1996 Founders Week Celebration with the Jameses,

Rev. Benjamin S. Foust of Bethel AME Church in Greensboro, North Carolina, in looking back on the life of Bishop and Mrs. James with a loud dignified inspirational voice recited.

THE LIVING FAITH

Bishop and Mrs. James:
You have dreamed many dreams that never came true.
You have seen them vanish at dawn, but you realized enough
of your dreams to make you want to dream on.

You have sown many seeds that fell by
the way, for the birds to feed upon,
But you have held enough golden sheaves in your hands
to make you want to sow on.

You prayed many prayers when no answer came, though you waited
patiently and long, but you have had answers of enough
of your prayers to make you want to pray on.

You trusted many friends, that failed and left you to cry alone;
but you had enough friends to ring true blue to make
you keep trusting on.

You drank the cup of disappointment and pain and have gone many
days without a song; but you tasted enough of the sweet
nectar of life to make you want to go on.

— by Rev. Benjamin S. Foust

This is dedicated to the life of Bishop Frederick Calhoun James as a servant of God, reconciler, father, healer, educator, prophet, civil rights leader, traditionalist in African Methodism, and loyal husband, and to his wife of more than 50 years Dr. Teressa Gregg James, a mother, great missionary, educator and doer. To God be the Glory for the things He has done and also for those He will continue to do through them. **TO GOD BE THE GLORY**

BIBLIOGRAPHY

_____, *The Holy Bible*, King James Version. World Bible Publishers: Iowa Falls.

_____, *The Holy Bible*, Today's English Version. American Bible Society: New York, 1978.

_____, *South Carolina District, Special Issue* "The Case for the Return of Bishop F. C. James to South Carolina." Seventh Episcopal District of the African Methodist Episcopal Church, June, 1992.

African Methodist Episcopal Church, *The Book of Discipline*, Forty-Fourth Edition. AMEC Sunday School Union: Nashville, TN, 1988.

James, Bishop Frederick, *African Methodism of South Carolina, A Bicentennial Focus*. Custombook, Inc.: New York, 1987

Metze, Charles II (narrator/writer); Harris, Layne (producer), "The Visionary Leader." Three Star Television.

Primary Sources:

Interviews: Bishop Frederick James, Mrs. Theressa Gregg James, Second District of AME Church presiding Elders and Ministers.

ABOUT THE AUTHOR

Rev. Dr. Mankekolo Mahlangu-Ngcobo is a native of South Africa. She is the first Black South African woman to receive a doctor of Ministry degree.

While in South Africa she taught at Seoding Elementary School, trained as a nurse and midwife at Baragwanath Hospital, and attended University of the North (Turfloop).

She has been involved in anti-Apartheid movements in South Africa and in exile (Canada and U.S.A.). She was detained and held in solitary confinement in South Africa.

She fled South Africa in 1980 and came to the United States of America in 1981. She was able to return to South Africa in 1991 to lead the National Coordinating Council for Repatriation (NCCR) of South African Exiles.

In the U.S. she received four degrees: BS degree (Magna Cum Laude) Morgan State University; Master of Public

Health, The Johns Hopkins University; Masters of Arts (Theology), St. Mary's University and Seminary, all in Baltimore, Maryland; and Seminary and Doctor of Ministry, United Theological Seminary in Dayton, Ohio.

She is presently an Associate Minister at Metropolitan A.M.E. Church in Washington, D.C. and a lecturer at Morgan State University in Baltimore, Maryland. She's also the author of several books.